Music for Flute & Piano

ADVANCED LEVEL
Volume 2

ISBN 978-1-59615-302-8

Music Minus One

EXCLUSIVELY DISTRIBUTED BY

HAL•LEONARD®

7777 W. BLUEMOUND RD. P.O. BOX 13819 MILWAUKEE, WI 53213

Visit Hal Leonard Online at
www.halleonard.com

PERFORMANCE GUIDE
COMMENTARY BY JULIUS BAKER AND MARTHA REARICK

BACH
Sonata in G Minor, 1st Movement (Allegro)

This piece has many interesting contrapuntal devices which should be made clear. Notice the interchange between flute and accompaniment. In measure 25, the flute plays material which the accompaniment copies in measure 29. The flute (in measure 29) takes the accompaniment figure. Do not overstress the repeated B flats here. They are a pedal point, and will be heard easily even if they are not emphasized. You will probably need to breathe on tied notes. Be careful that your breathing does not leave holes in the line. The material beginning in measure 74 is an excellent opportunity to play long, smooth, legato lines. The flute has the accompaniment figure again in measure 108; listen carefully to the theme in the piano part. This music is well worth the practice it will take!

MOZART
Concerto in G Major, K. 313, 1st Movement (Allegro maestoso)

This very florid movement must be practiced slowly and evenly. You must resist the temptation to go too fast too soon. The sixteenth notes must be clear, even, and never feel rushed or hurried. When you get to the second theme (after letter B) you will want a more lyric quality to contrast with the martial quality of the first theme. The little trills in the development section are very difficult. If you try to trill too much on the little eighth note pick-up, you will hold the tempo back. Just play a mordent; that will be embellishment enough at the performance tempo! When you have big intervals, you will have to bring out the low notes and subdue the high ones. There is almost no rallentando before the recapitulation at letter D. Do not rush the triplets in this section. Notice the articulation at letter E. You will want to slur the sixteenth notes in groups of two's.

Editor's Note: It is customary to insert a cadenza in the final tutti. The following cadenza is by Ary van Leeuwen:

FAURE
Fantasie, Op. 79

If you play this Andantino too slowly, you will lose the long phrases. Notice how the theme returns in measures 25 and 26. You will want to stress the notes with the stems up so that the melody is easily heard. The thirty second notes will be easier if you remember that they are embellishments. In measure 35, the ensemble will be better if you do not start the run (after the low C) too soon. Be sure you have enough air to give these phrases full support; you will need a breath after the high E in measure 36.

The Allegro is bright and cheerful. You will need to use double tonguing. If you use a "duh-guh" syllable, the tone will not be too percussive. When you enter after a sixteenth rest, as in measure 74, you will have to be careful that you are not late. This will also be a danger after tied notes. The quarter note triplets in measures 99 and 100 must be properly spaced. If you change your thinking to a pulse of one in measures 97 and 98, the triplets should not trouble you. The low passage beginning with the second beat of measure 112 is the most difficult in the piece. After the very high B natural in measure 111, you will have to think ahead and work to loosen your embouchure. The *espressivo* beginning in measure 117 needs a singing tone with a lot of vibrato. You will need to double tongue the section beginning in measure 151. Play as loudly as you can so that the chord in the accompaniment doesn't cover you.

Give the high B flat in measure 159 just a hint of vibrato so that it has good quality. If you are not careful, these high notes will sound like chalk on a blackboard! You will need to double-tongue again in measure 176. The accompaniment has the melodic interest in the *leggiero* section, beginning in measure 192. If you remember that you are playing an obligato made up of embellished chords, this section will be easier. You can use regular fingering in measure 230. If you give the final note just a tiny vibrato, it will have a better sound.

Julius Baker
Martha Rearick

CONTENTS

SONATA

J. S. BACH

CONCERTO NO. 1 K. 313

The audio tracks for this piece begin at measure 19.

WOLFGANG A. MOZART

♩ = 110 (7'09")

12

FANTASIE

GABRIEL FAURE
Op. 79

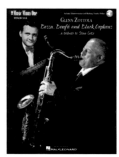